a **S**pecial **G**ift **f**or

Sue

with **l**ove

Mary Ahyberg

date

10-31-2010

Stories, sayings, and scriptures to Encourage and Inspire

hugs™
for
Gardeners

HOWARD BOOKS
A DIVISION OF SIMON & SCHUSTER
New York   London   Toronto   Sydney

TAMMY L. BICKET AND DAWN M. BRANDON
PERSONALIZED SCRIPTURES BY
LEANN WEISS

For our dads

Our purpose at Howard Books is to:
Increase faith in the hearts of growing Christians
Inspire holiness in the lives of believers
Instill hope in the hearts of struggling people everywhere
Because He's coming again!

HOWARD
BOOKS

Published by Howard Books, a division of Simon & Schuster, Inc.
1230 Avenue of the Americas, New York, NY 10020
www.howardpublishing.com

Hugs for Gardeners © 2007 by Tammy L. Bicket and Dawn M. Brandon

ISBN 13: 978-1-4165-4179-0
ISBN 10:   1-4165-4179-9
ISBN 13: 978-1-58229-697-5 (gift edition)
ISBN 10:   1-58229-697-9 (gift edition)

10   9   8   7   6   5   4   3   2   1

HOWARD colophon is a registered trademark of Simon & Schuster, Inc.

Manufactured in the United States of America

For information regarding special discounts for bulk purchases, please contact: Simon & Schuster Special Sales at 1-800-456-6798 or business@simonandschuster.com.

Edited by Chrys Howard
Cover design by John Mark Luke Designs
Interior design by Tennille Paden

Paraphrased scriptures © 2007 LeAnn Weiss, 3006 Brandywine Drive, Orlando, FL 32806; 407-898-4410

Unless otherwise noted, Scripture quotations are taken from the *Holy Bible, New International Version*; copyright © 1973, 1978, 1984 by International Bible Society; used by permission of Zondervan; all rights reserved. Scripture quotations marked MSG are taken from *The Message*; copyright © 1993, 1994, 1995, 1996, 2000, 2001, 2002; used by permission of NavPress Publishing Group.

Contents

Chapter 1

Heirloom Gardening

When you draw close to Me, you'll always discover a connection. My kingdom and My love are constant for all generations. No matter what your circumstances in life, you can always count on Me. I'll never leave you or neglect you. I'm 100 percent faithful in all My promises, and loving toward you.

Loving you always,
Your Everlasting God

—from James 4:8; Psalm 100:5; Deuteronomy 31:8;
Psalm 145:13

The new big thing in gardening is something old—heirlooms. Variety is part of the appeal of growing heirloom plants. Imagine growing tomatoes as small as your fingertip or weighing as much as two pounds each, colored various shades of red, yellow, white, purple, pink, orange, green, or even striped. How about eggplants with tiny fruits that look like green peas, or pole beans with red pods that grow up to two feet long?

Now consider the joy of knowing that eighty years ago, Great-grandmother worked the soil to grow those same varieties and lovingly stirred them into soups and stews that fed the family and nurtured the collective soul as they were handed down as favorite family recipes. Perhaps the best part about growing heirlooms (besides the great taste) is the glimpse they offer into the past—the connection with those who have gone before us.

Whether you save seeds and grow heirlooms or buy plants from the local nursery, gardening is about connections—to the earth, to deep parts within yourself, to the past and the future. You may be an old pro from a long line of gardeners who passed on their wisdom or a neophyte just tentatively starting your first little plot. It doesn't matter. You're now connected, embraced. You are benefiting from what some family member or gardener did in the past. Treasure that connection, that link with the past. Remember it. Live worthy of those who have prepared the ground before you. And take care to pass along to another generation that special sense of relationship and interdependence that reminds us we belong to something bigger than ourselves.

Gardening is a habit of which I hope never to be cured,
one shared with an array of fascinating people who helped
me grow and bloom among my flowers.

Martha Smith

the Family Garden

Five-year-old Kate awoke with anticipation shortly after the sun came up, as she did each Saturday morning, and lay very still, listening for her father's stirrings downstairs. If she held her breath and listened hard, she would just be able to hear the coffeemaker gurgling its cheery preparations. And that's when Daddy would be sitting at the kitchen table, reading the morning paper.

Beeeep! The coffeemaker sounded. That was Kate's cue. She scrambled out of bed with excitement and raced to put on her special "garden clothes." She stuffed her mass of curly red locks through the neck hole of her dirt-stained, favorite shirt. It was the pale yellow one with terra-cotta pots and bright gerbera daisies in red, pink, and orange on the front. Then she'd pull on the denim jeans worn thin at the knees and reinforced with patches of heavy material her mother had cut in the shapes of garden tools.

Appropriately attired, Kate slipped downstairs as quietly as possible so Mom wouldn't hear. Kate didn't want to waste any of her special time on things like brushing her teeth or having her hair put in pigtails.

Carefully avoiding all the creaky spots on the stairs as only a wispy little girl could do, Kate finally reached the bottom and peered around the corner.

There sat Daddy, just as he did every Saturday morning. And just like every Saturday morning, he looked up from his coffee and paper and gave his little girl a smile that made her giggle and run over for her morning hug.

"Good morning, Katie-girl," he always said as he pulled her into his lap. "Let's go see what's growing in the garden today."

The two headed outside, stopping by the storage shed to get the proper equipment: man-size gloves and garden tools for him, child-size gloves and tools for Kate.

In the spring they would work together to plant the garden. Everything had been started from seed months earlier. Her dad prepared the starter pots in his workshop in the basement. Kate would drop in the seeds and help water and care for them as they sprouted and grew. But she never could bring herself to do the thinning—pulling out the smaller plants so the larger ones would grow big and tall. Sensitive to his little girl's gentle nature, her dad never discarded the little sprouts. He always replanted them in their own soil so they could thrive as well.

Kate thought the little seedlings looked so small and lonely in their bigger pots instead of all together, but Dad had patiently explained that the separation was necessary for the plants to have enough room to grow to be strong and healthy.

Planting the garden was Kate's favorite time because her dad would recite the stories that went with each item.

With the planting of the tomatoes, onions, and peppers, Dad would tell of when he was a little boy growing up on a small farm and working side by side with his father in their large garden. He still used the same heirloom varieties his dad had used all those years ago. In fact, he had started the garden from seeds his father passed on to him when he married Momma and started his first garden.

The summer squash and zucchini were descended from Grandpa's garden too, and Dad would tell stories of how he would harvest and sell them at his little roadside stand to earn money for a bike when he was not much older than Kate.

The back row of the garden was always reserved for a very

special crop—Grandma's hollyhocks. Grandma had come to America from Denmark when she was a young girl, and her mother had brought hollyhock seeds with her as a reminder of her homeland. Grandma always took great pride in the hollyhocks and would get misty-eyed telling stories of when she was a little girl in a faraway land.

After she was gone, Dad (who had never bothered much with flowers) took special interest and pride in planting hollyhocks in his garden. The first year after Grandma died, he and Kate had held a special, ceremonial planting. He knew how much she missed her grandma, and he took extra time that day to tell her all the stories he could remember about his mother and her life.

Kate's favorite part of the garden, however, were the bright red dahlias that lined the front. She especially liked the dahlias because of a picture she had seen of her dad. About six years old and with a mass of curls she could tell were red even in the black-and-white photo, young Bill was squatting down tending dahlias whose blooms were nearly as big as his freckled face. It was a tangible evidence of the connection she felt with her dad in the garden.

Those years seemed long ago and yet so close to Kate's heart that she ached. Her husband, Jerry, had been transferred to an office in Indiana, far from her Virginia roots, and they were just settling into their new home. They had chosen the house and property largely because Kate fell in love with it the moment she saw it. The large, restored, two-story farmhouse sat on five acres of gently rolling land. With its cheery kitchen and quaint style, it seemed to Kate to embody the sentiment of her family history. There was even a large garden in the backyard.

Kate had waited with eager anticipation for the spring thaw so she could plant. She'd gone to a local greenhouse and picked out several healthy plants, purchased some sturdy tools, and prepared the ground.

But now, as she stood looking out her kitchen window at the empty garden and waiting for the coffee to brew and the sun to warm the dew-covered ground, she felt so sad she could barely swallow the lump in her throat. Her eyes welled up and then overflowed with tears as she gave in to the loneliness she felt being so far away from everything she knew. She didn't know if she could bear planting a garden without her dad by her side.

A creak behind her made her choke back her tears, and she struggled to regain her composure. Wiping her wet cheeks as discreetly as she could, Kate turned around to see a mass of curly red locks coming down the stairs. Her little boy rounded the corner and gleefully ran to the kitchen, throwing his chubby little arms around Kate's legs.

"Mommy, are we going to plant the garden today? It's Saturday, and you promised."

Kate couldn't resist his boyish enthusiasm. "Yes," she said, smiling in spite of her heartache. "Come on, Billy, let's get started."

Mother and son were retrieving their tools from the storage shed when Kate thought she heard the doorbell. *Oh well,* she thought. *Surely Jerry will be up by now and will see who it is.* She and Billy put on their work gloves. She loved watching him struggle to get them on, dressed in his ragged jeans and the new shirt she had bought him with a hoe, rake, and shovel on the front.

"Kate!" she heard from a distance. "Kate, a package just arrived for you." Jerry was walking toward her from the house.

"What is it?" she asked, curious. "I'm not expecting anything."

"I don't know," Jerry said with a shrug. "Let's open it and see."

Using one blade of her garden shears, Kate cut through the packing tape and pulled back the flaps of the box—and then she couldn't breathe. Tears flooded back to her eyes, and she had to bite her lip to stifle the sob that nearly escaped. Inside the carefully packed box was an assortment of vegetable plants and some envelopes of seeds. She knew immediately who must have sent them. *Oh, Daddy,* she cried silently.

Included in each envelope of bulbs and seeds was a sheet of paper. Her father had written down the stories that went with each kind—except for one. In the envelope with dahlia bulbs, there was no note—only a black-and-white photo of a little boy tending big, red dahlias.

"There's a note," Jerry said, handing Kate another envelope. Kate opened it and read.

Dearest Katie-girl,

I know it's difficult for you to be so far away, and I will miss your company in the garden. But I've sent you some special plants so you'll always feel close in heart and always have a reminder of our special times together.

Remember when you were a little girl and thought the seedlings looked lonely all by themselves in a big pot and how I explained that it was necessary for them to grow healthy and strong? Sometimes life is like that, Katie. I know you feel lonely being separated from everything you grew up knowing. But sometimes we need our own plot of ground to find out just how wonderful and strong we can become.

You've grown into a strong but gentle and loving woman, Katie-girl. I'm proud of you. It's time to thrive in your own place. But always know that you're never really far from your roots—or from my heart.

Love,
Daddy

"Mommy," Billy tugged on her pant leg. "Can we start now?"

Kate sat down cross-legged on the ground with her little boy and handed him a tomato plant. "Let me tell you a story . . ."

Chapter 2

Propagating Wisdom

Teach My standards of living. Remember . . . your life is an example to others. When you're short of wisdom, ask Me and I'll generously enrich you. Teach others with integrity. Let your words be beyond reproach. Do they pass My higher wisdom test? Are they pure, peace-loving, considerate, submissive, full of mercy and good fruit, impartial, and sincere?

Leading by example,
Your God of All Wisdom

—from Titus 2:1–8; James 1:5, 3:17

Have you ever met a Master Gardener? The title is more than just a compliment: it's an official designation recognized throughout the United States and Canada—and it's hard earned! Master Gardeners have invested many hours of intensive training in home-gardening techniques. These folks really know what they're doing. They're experts in soil preparation, planting, propagating, cultivating, staking, composting, plant and pest identification, problem solving, and anything else you might have questions about regarding your garden. They take classes, attend seminars, and get hands-on training every year. It's a major commitment.

But learning the secrets of gardening for themselves is only half of what it means to be a Master Gardener. The other half involves passing on the wisdom of their experience and knowledge to others. They are avid community volunteers. They help university agricultural extensions with research and by giving lectures and demonstrations, exhibiting displays, coordinating school and community gardening projects, and manning phone lines so stumped gardeners can call for answers and advice.

Kind of sounds like a parent: forever learning, always teaching.

Even if you're not a parent, others need answers only you can provide. You have the experience, the wisdom, and the understanding heart to size up a situation and help find a reasonable solution. You may not know everything, but as long as you're committed to learning from *the* Master Gardener, you know enough to make a positive difference in someone's life. Someone—your child, a friend, the woman who cuts your hair, a neighbor—is looking for answers today. Won't you share what you know?

To create a little flower is the labour of ages.

William Blake

What the Master Gardener Knew

Something big was brewing with Sommer. Why else would a nineteen-year-old just home from her first year of college be out in the garden early Saturday morning, helping her mom tie up tomato plants? As a Master Gardener sworn to teach others the joys and mysteries of gardening, Fran had long dreamed of sharing her wisdom and love of growing things with her children, but none of the three seemed to catch the bug that had bitten her in childhood. Fran was not so naive as to think such an interest had finally awakened in her oldest child.

Sommer had never volunteered to work in the garden unless something was troubling her. Work that needed to be done was the surest way to find Mom alone. As the smell of cookies baking inexorably drew the brood like a powerful magnet, work repelled them just as strongly. It made such chores the perfect time for heart-to-heart talks.

Despite the idyllic early-summer day and the hypnotic drone of an airplane flying high overhead, Fran sensed her daughter's agitation. It unnerved her more than usual. After all, Sommer was growing up. Her problems and concerns were bigger now, more complicated, not so easy for a parent to solve. Plus, Sommer had been gone most of the past eight months. Eighty miles wasn't too great a distance when Sommer needed money, clean clothes, or some of mom's home-baked goodies, but it might as well have been a thousand miles in the way it had managed to shut Fran out of the little things that made up her daughter's everyday life. That realization had often made her sad.

Now it made her nervous. Calmly wrapping the nylon around the stake and the Early Girl plant Sommer was dutifully holding, Fran waited for her daughter to feel comfortable unburdening her heart. Fran's mind raced to a million possibilities, from the mundane (Sommer was having problems with her flighty roommate) to the more serious (she had a stalker or had gotten preg—). *No!* Fran firmly rejected the thought. She trusted Sommer and felt guilty for entertaining such a notion.

Maybe she wouldn't sound like an untrusting, desperate mother if she asked a few general, nonjudgmental questions, just to get things started.

"Anything you want to talk about?" Fran asked.

So much for subtlety. She watched Sommer's brow furrow darkly and hoped she hadn't been too bold.

"That obvious, is it?"

"I know a few things about life . . . about you," Fran stopped tying and studied Sommer's face. "Is it Todd?" she ventured cautiously, suddenly somehow sure it was.

Sommer's face registered surprise. "How did you know? I thought I'd been acting like everything was fine."

Fran laughed. "Maybe you're not such a great actor."

"Yeah, well, I hope Todd is," Sommer grumbled half beneath her breath. But Fran caught it, as she knew Sommer had intended, and now Fran had a pretty good idea of what Sommer was wrestling with.

"He's seriously thinking about going to Hollywood?" Fran asked softly.

"He thinks he has a really good shot at making a name for himself." The next words tumbled from Sommer's mouth in a torrent. "You know how everyone always says how much he looks like Jake Gyllenhaal. And his aunt *was* in those commercials for Healthy Glo Pool and Spa, and everyone said she had star quality . . . and Todd's a lot like her. He showed me an article that said it's easier than ever for good-looking guys with talent to break into acting with a good agent, and he got an agent who's worked with lots of big names. He said Todd has what it takes, and he'll help him get there, and . . . it all sounds great, doesn't it?"

Fran took a deep breath before responding.

"That sounds like what Todd wants to believe. But it seems to me that you're not really buying it. You're smart and have good instincts. This is making you nervous for good reasons."

"But what about Todd's instincts? He really believes he can make this work."

"Like his comic-book idea that Marvel Comics was sure to buy . . . or his rap songs?" Fran gently reminded Sommer of the first of Todd's failed enterprises that came to mind. Sommer deflated a little but seemed resistant.

"There's more to this than just Todd's going to California, isn't there?" Fran prodded gently. She was almost afraid to ask the question but was increasingly convinced it was the heart of Sommer's real dilemma: "Is he trying to get you to go with him?"

"I *am* going with him, Mama," Sommer said softly but firmly, her eyes and the set of her jaw announcing that her mind was made up.

Fran's heart fell. "What about college . . . what will you live on? Do you have any kind of workable plan?" Fran tried to stay cool. She didn't want to put Sommer on the defensive, further hardening her resolve.

Sommer put her hand reassuringly on her mother's shoulder. "Mom, you've always taught me to think things through and have a plan, so yes, I know what I'm doing. I've got a little money in savings that should hold us until I get a job—I'm a good waitress. I'll get one."

"Do you know how much it'll cost just for gas to get out there?" Fran said, interrupting her. "Or how high rent is for even the most basic apartment in that area? And you're not even married, which further complicates the . . . you're not . . ." Fran was growing more frantic.

"No! We're not married! And don't worry, Mom, I'm not going to compromise my moral standards. I know stuff's expensive. But there's always my college fund— Don't spaz out, Mom." Sommer talked over her mother's expression of dismay and alarm. "It would just be temporary. I wouldn't be going to school for a year or so, but it wouldn't take long for Todd to be making enough money from television and movies to repay that money and put me through school."

"But Sommer," Fran protested, "your dream of being a veterinarian . . ."

"I'm not giving it up," Sommer said vehemently. "Besides, L.A. has some great colleges: UCLA, Loyola Marymount . . .

and if I live there for a year, I'll get the in-state tuition rates."

Fran bit her lip, partly to keep from crying, partly to keep from saying something she'd regret—something that could cause an irreparable rift in their relationship.

"I'm an adult, Mom. I don't need your permission to do this, but your blessing would be nice."

"But I can't say I approve of this at all." Fran sighed. "I don't understand how you can believe this is in your best interest."

"I guess there's a lot you don't understand," Sommer said hotly. "My future is about more than books and a career. I don't know if Todd can make it in Hollywood or not . . . it's a long shot . . . the timing isn't what I'd hoped for, but we all make compromises to—*iyeaah!*" Sommer ducked her head, jumped backward, and waved her arms in front of her face.

Startled, Fran heard it too, the loud buzz of a bee close by. She empathized with her daughter but found her contortions comical. "Relax," she chuckled, "it's a carpenter bee; it won't hurt you."

"It's the biggest bee I've ever seen!" Sommer squealed as she danced around the garden. "It's bigger than my thumb, and it's flying right at my head! What do you mean it won't hurt me?"

"It's a male; he's guarding the bee chambers in the shed's overhang. They're huge, aggressive defenders, but they don't have stingers. It's all bluff and bluster."

"You're sure?" Sommer stopped hopping and waving, but still crouched defensively.

"I'm sure." Fran had a sudden insight. "Come here."

"What?" Sommer approached, now curious.

"A tomato hornworm is eating one of these plants. Can you find it for me?"

Intrigued, Sommer scanned the tomatoes for a moment, then plunged wholeheartedly into the search. "Do *you* see it?" she asked, moving branches and looking carefully.

"Not yet, but I know where to find it. You're getting farther away from it—that's better . . . warmer, warmer . . . *wait!* Right there!"

Sommer peered intently at the leaves before her but obviously still saw nothing.

"Lift the leaf," Fran urged.

"Ewwwwww!" Sommer recoiled.

Fran pried the four-inch-long green caterpillar from the tomato, then tossed it in a pail of soapy water. "One of these can strip a plant bare in just a day or two."

"That's disgusting!" Sommer groaned. "How did you know it was there?"

"A little knowledge and a lot of experience. Those things blend right in and look like the plant. I know the signs to look for—eaten leaves, droppings—that alert me to the danger and lead me right to the culprit."

Sommer was silent, but she looked thoughtful, so Fran continued. "Honey, I think maybe you're afraid that if you don't go to California, you'll lose Todd." Sommer's eyes grew moist, and she swallowed hard. "But acting on that fear is like dancing with the carpenter bee. What you should be afraid of is more subtle but more destructive in the long term, like the hornworm. Do you know how hard it is to go back to school after quitting? Have you thought about what it'll be like without all your friends and family nearby—your support system? Don't let Todd's bluster distract you from safeguarding yourself against choices that could truly destroy your future." With that, Fran turned back to her gardening. She had given Sommer something to think about. Now it was up to her.

The rain had finally let up, and Fran stood on the porch, pulling on her garden shoes. She was anxious to check the rain gauge and inspect the garden.

"Can I go with you?" Sommer joined her tentatively on the porch. After nearly a week of Sommer's avoiding her, Fran wondered if this might be a continuation of their last garden conversation.

They walked silently as Fran waited for her daughter to speak. The long pause felt awkward.

"I'm not going to California."

Fran felt a rush of relief. "Did Todd change his mind?"

"No." That pause again. "But I did."

Fran put her arm around Sommer's shoulders and squeezed affectionately. "Thank you," she whispered.

"I didn't do it for you," Sommer protested. "I did it for me . . . and, well, *because* of you."

Fran looked at her curiously.

"I pretty much decided that you know more than I sometimes give you credit for—like with the bee, and that horrible bug! I know Todd's scheme is unrealistic, and the consequences of following him are all too real—even if I can't see them all in advance. I have a pretty good idea you can, and you want what's best for me."

Fran's eyes glistened with joy and gratitude for such a wise, teachable daughter. But then she'd known that, too.

Chapter 3

Planting Seeds of Compassion

*S*ow righteousness, reap the fruit of unfailing love, and soften your heart to seek Me. Realize that when you sow in tears, you'll eventually reap songs of joy. Start with your faith. Then plant the seeds of goodness, knowledge, self-control, perseverance, godliness, kindness, and love. If you keep growing in these qualities, your life won't be ineffective or unproductive in what really counts.

Purposefully blossoming you,
Your Creator

—*from Hosea 10:12; Psalm 126:5–6; 2 Peter 1:5–8*

If you want to grow pretty flowers, plant marigolds, not horseradish. If you prefer the smell of perfume rather than sewage, plant lavender, not cabbages. If you want flowers that will reseed themselves, growing back year after year, plant dianthus or hollyhocks.

It may be stating the obvious to an accomplished gardener like yourself, but the seeds you sow are extremely important. Galatians 6:7–8 says: "What a person plants, he will harvest. The person who plants selfishness, ignoring the needs of others—ignoring God!—harvests a crop of weeds. All he'll have to show for his life is weeds! But the one who plants in response to God, letting God's Spirit do the growth work in him, harvests a crop of real life" (MSG).

When it comes to dealing

with others, what kind of seeds are you sowing? Are you sowing seeds of selfishness, bitterness, or self-protection? Or are you sowing seeds of compassion and kindness? Both kinds of seeds are sure to grow and produce a crop. But only one crop is worth the effort, producing a harvest of community, support, and love.

Have a difficult boss or an annoying neighbor? Plant seeds of politeness, respect, and joy that will choke out the seeds of strife. A family member loses his temper at you? Crowd out the seeds of hatred by sowing seeds of quietness and restraint. You not only might change those people but also plant seeds of compassion in the lives of those who are watching your conduct—especially your children.

Isn't that a crop worth sowing?

The person who sows seeds of kindness enjoys a perpetual harvest.

Anonymous

the Sunshine House

"Megan, did you find it?" Bob called, leaning on his shovel. His ten-year-old daughter came running from the neighboring yard, carrying her yellow-handled trowel.

"Yeah," she said breathlessly. "I must've left it in Granny May's yard yesterday when I helped her plant petunias."

May and Frank Reichner had lived in the house next door since he'd come back from World War II and bought it, thanks to the GI Bill. Bob always sensed some residual military discipline about the man. Though he was pleasant enough, he wasn't the type to "adopt" grandchildren, as his wife did with Megan. "How many times have I told you not to leave your stuff over there? Mr. Reichner doesn't like things to look cluttered, and you don't want Granny May to trip on them."

Megan nodded impatiently. "Can we plant now?"

Bob chuckled. Megan had been waiting to plant her sunflowers since she had refused to put down the packet in the seed store three weeks ago. "They're like sunshine," she'd insisted. "I want to plant them *everywhere*!" They had negotiated down to a somewhat smaller area.

"Yes, we can plant now."

Bob had spent the morning preparing the ground along both sides of the sidewalk. They'd plant one long row of sunflowers on each side of the walk. He helped Megan bring the plants they'd started in peat pots and arrange them twelve inches apart all along the path.

"How long till they bloom?" she asked when they were almost finished.

"What does the packet say?"

She read with concentration. "When started from seed, ger . . ."

"Germination. That's when the seeds sprout, so we've already done that. Let's see. . . ." He read the envelope for the first time

himself. "Days to maturity, seventy. . . . Ten to twelve feet tall."
Ten to twelve feet tall?! He looked at the house and sidewalk,
then at Sandy, who'd emerged from the house and now stood
giggling at her husband's shock. "It'll be like walking through
a tunnel!"

Sandy looked as gleeful as Megan. "We'll have a tunnel of
sunshine! We'll be the Sunshine House on Sunshine Lane!"

The sunflowers grew and bloomed, and Megan was thrilled.
She led Granny May by the hand up and down the lane, both
oohing and ahhing in perfect delight. "It's just like when I was a
little girl," May said dreamily. Soon even neighbors were calling
their home the Sunshine House. Everyone commented on how
lovely and cheerful it was.

Except Frank.

At first he'd just walk by and harrumph. Then he started
making little comments. "Those things are awfully tall." Mostly
he just grumbled and moved on. But one day he caught Bob
when he was edging the lawn.

Bob couldn't hear much of what he said, but he could tell
from the look on Frank's face that he wasn't happy. He cut the
motor on the edger. "Sorry?"

"I said, How long are you gonna keep those things there?"
He gestured toward the sunflowers.

"Oh . . . uh . . . well, I think they'll last until fall."

"They're blocking my view."

"Excuse me?"

"I can't see around the corner when I'm driving. It's dangerous."

Bob looked over at the rows. They *would* be in the line of vision when driving on the street. But it was pretty easy to see between them. Frank was just getting too cantankerous. A few days ago he had scolded Sandy for letting Megan make too much noise in the backyard. Still, May had always been sweet to them, and he didn't want to be at odds with his neighbors. He would tread carefully. "I'm sorry they bother you, Mr. Reichner. Maybe you could look between the stems to check for oncoming traffic. See?"

Frank went red in the face. "I'm not blind. I'm telling you they're in the way. And they look ridiculous. Who ever heard of planting sunflowers like that! I'm telling you, they have to go."

Bob felt his own face flush. "Frank, they're not endangering anyone's safety, and my family loves those sunflowers. I can't just cut them down."

His neighbor huffed and turned on his heels. "We'll see about that."

Bob decided to avoid Frank for a while, and he told Megan not to bother Granny May. She hadn't been outside chatting over the fence since earlier in the summer, and now it seemed clear why. Even if she didn't mind the flowers, her husband was furious about them, and she probably thought it best to just lay low. So that was the policy they'd all adopt.

Mid-July brought a heavy afternoon thunderstorm, and that evening as Bob retrieved the mail, he noticed Frank slowly picking up downed sticks and small limbs from his massive oak tree. He looked old and tired, and Bob felt a twinge of sympathy. Maybe he should help him. He walked into the house and laid the junk mail and bills on the kitchen counter. "What's this?" he asked when he spotted a certified, official-looking envelope.

"It's from an attorney," Sandy began cautiously, opening and scanning it. She took a deep breath. "Frank has filed a lawsuit over the sunflowers."

"He *what?*" The only thing that tempered Bob's anger was the growing realization of the implications. A legal fight would be expensive. *A court battle. Over sunflowers.* It was too absurd. He looked out the window to the Reichners' property, where Frank was still hunched over. *He can pick up sticks until he drops.*

The next morning, after breakfast, Bob looked out the window and couldn't believe his eyes. Mr. Reichner was right there on Bob's front porch. He was talking animatedly to May, who was sitting on the step. She seemed upset. *The nerve,* Bob fumed. He flung open the door, ready to let off steam. But the words caught in his throat.

May had crossed her arms stubbornly and seemed near hysteria. "I'm telling you, I live here and I'm not leaving."

Bob looked from May to Frank, and realized the man's

expression was less angry than flustered. When Frank spoke to May, his voice was tender and a little desperate. "Sweetheart, you don't live here. You're confused. Come on, let's go home."

"I *am* home," she insisted tearfully. "I live with the sunflowers."

"Try to remember, honey. You haven't lived with the sunflowers in more than fifty years. You're thinking of the old farmhouse. We live over there, see?" He pointed to their home, but May just turned her head away, refusing his pleas.

Frank rubbed his head in frustration. When he turned to face the house, Bob wasn't sure whether the man was going to hurl curses at him or break down and cry. Caught off guard, Bob stood with his mouth open. Suddenly all Frank's frustration seemed to bubble to the surface, and he bellowed, "You and your"—his voice broke and he waved his arms—*"sunflowers!"*

Bob took a step forward to try to comfort or help, but Frank waved him off. "Leave us alone," he hissed. "We'll be out of your hair in just a minute."

"Now, May, we have to go," he said firmly as he put his arm around her shoulders, half lifting her from her seated position. This time she gave in, and he walked her down the sidewalk and home.

"Mom, what's wrong with Granny May?" Megan asked quietly. Sandy and Megan had joined Bob on the porch. He looked at his wife and saw that she was as unsettled and saddened as he was. The scene they'd just witnessed explained a lot.

"It's okay, honey," Sandy said as she recovered her composure. "She probably doesn't feel well and just got a little confused. Come inside and eat your breakfast."

Bob plopped on the couch. He was still thinking about the incident when Sandy sat down beside him. "Wow," she sighed. "Poor May."

"Yeah. And poor Frank." He put his arm around his wife. "I can't imagine what it would be like to watch the person you love slipping away and not be able to do anything about it. No wonder he's grumpy."

"Dad," Megan said, coming from the kitchen with grape jelly still on her cheek, "can we plant more sunflowers in little pots?"

"I think we have enough," Bob said, wiping her face with his thumb.

"Do you think we could plant some in Granny May's yard? Maybe that would make her happy."

Bob drew a deep breath. "That's a good idea, honey." He paused. "But I'm not sure Mr. Reichner really wants sunflowers in his yard."

"Can we ask him tomorrow?"

"We'll see. Now go wash your face and get dressed."

"They sprouted, Daddy!" Megan danced in excitement. "Granny May's sunflowers. Can we plant them now?"

"We can ask. But it's up to Mr. Reichner, and you can't press him, okay?"

They headed next door, where Frank was picking up another windfall of sticks. May was sitting on the front porch.

"Mr. Reichner, look!" Megan thrust the seedlings out for his appraisal. "They're sunflowers. I planted them for Granny. I thought she'd like to have some in her yard. Then you can have a sunshine house, too!"

Frank was clearly taken aback.

"Megan, why don't you go sit with Granny for a minute," Bob urged. He turned to Frank. "She, uh . . . just wants to help. I told her you may not want sunflowers."

His elderly neighbor swallowed and looked at the ground, but Bob had seen the gathering tears. "She . . . gets confused. More than she used to." He looked toward his wife. "If I don't watch her, she wanders right off." He shuffled his feet and bent down stiffly for more sticks. "Like the other day."

Bob wasn't good at this. He never knew what to say. He started picking up sticks and adding them to Frank's bag.

"She used to live on a farm out near North Platte. Lots of sunflowers up by the house."

"Must have been lovely."

Frank nodded.

They were quiet for a few minutes. Bob wasn't sure whether to stay or go. "I'd be happy to bring my mulcher over, chop these things up," he said, glancing at the sticks.

Frank didn't answer. "About your sunflowers . . ." He nodded toward Sunshine Lane. Bob tensed. "I can mostly see through 'em if I look real careful."

Bob tried to hide a smile. "Well . . . maybe next year we can plant a shorter variety."

"Nah," Frank said, still not venturing eye contact. "You wanna stick with these. Make better seeds."

"You know how to collect and roast the seeds? Would you show me?"

Frank worked his mouth thoughtfully. "Might." He paused and looked toward their tidy white house. "If you'll help Megan and me plant those seedlings o' hers by the back porch there. Might make May feel more at home." He watched May and Megan, chatting happily, stroll over toward Sunshine Lane.

Bob grinned and watched, too. "Yeah," he said, "I think we can do that."

Chapter 4

Transplanting

Trust Me! I am able to take the things others meant for your harm and change them into your opportunities for growth. Watch Me do far beyond all that you can ask or dream. When you delight in My ways and meditate on My Word, you'll be like a tree firmly planted by living water. You'll see abundant results in My perfect time. I'll multiply all that you do. Remember, nothing is too difficult for Me! It might not make sense right now . . . just remember that through the disappointments and struggles, I'm changing you into a reflection of My Glory.

For you, today and always,
Your God of All Hope

—from Romans 8:28; Ephesians 3:20; Psalm 1:1–3;
Jeremiah 32:17; 2 Corinthians 4:16

Almost every gardener has experience transplanting specimens at one time or another. Whether you buy young plants at the nursery to transplant into the garden, start your own from seed, or merely move an already-established plant to a more spacious, better-suited location, you understand the concept of transplanting.

From the plant's perspective, transplanting might seem a terrible option. Imagine leaving the climate-controlled environment of the greenhouse for uncertain conditions outdoors. Too much sun might scald you. Too little or too much rain could doom you. Strong winds bend or break you while animals, insects, or even a careless gardener can inflict devastating damage.

Given the stresses involved in transplanting, it might seem better to leave a plant where it is. But every gardener knows the

benefits of transplanting: the warmth of
the sun to grow strong by, deeper soil for
more sustenance, and more room to spread and
grow.

Did you know that when a plant outgrows its
place, if it's not transplanted quickly enough, its
growth might be forever stunted? When vegetables become root-bound, chemical messengers
signal them to stop growing. Transplanting at
the right time is key to growing large, healthy,
productive plants. It's the same with people.

When you find yourself suddenly uprooted
and out of your element, remember the lesson
of transplantation. Change is difficult, but
often essential. You may not have chosen
it, but the Master Gardener has. Trust
that He knows what He's doing. He
has prepared this place for you;
now put down your roots, turn
your face toward the Son,
and grow!

Life begins the day you start a garden.

Chinese proverb

the Victory Garden

Shanti awoke in the fetal position, tightly clutching a pillow to her chest. For a moment she couldn't quite pinpoint the cause of the grief and horror that threatened to engulf her, but understanding soon returned like the tide.

They'd fired her . . . out of the blue . . . for no good reason save that she was a little too passionate about the work, raised the bar a little too high to suit the comfort of administrators who cared more about maintaining the status quo and protecting their own turf than they cared about the people they served and the aid organization whose goals they ostensibly worked to further. She hadn't been their enemy, but it turned out they'd been hers for years.

It still shocked her and made her angry at herself that she hadn't seen it coming. But worse, she felt like a part of her—an arm, both legs, her heart—had been viciously ripped away. She had loved her mission, the people she worked with, those she served. She had put everything—absolutely everything—into doing the best job she possibly could. And she'd been highly successful. Too successful. *What kind of a place penalizes success?* Shanti mourned. *How could God let them do this to me when I was making a positive contribution? It mattered. I mattered. And now it's gone.*

It was 9:47. Break time. Would everyone be talking about it, or would they keep silent, afraid they might be next? What were people saying and thinking since she couldn't be there to defend herself against their phony nobility disguised as concern for her privacy, making her look guilty of some unknown heinous offense while precluding any explanation or defense of their heartless action. How would the work suffer?

The heartsickness she felt was compounded by fear: after fifteen years of service, they'd given her almost no severance, and their charitable-organization status had made them exempt from paying unemployment insurance—so she'd draw no compensation. But in spite of her impending financial disaster, she felt too beaten up, too fragile to look for work. Besides, what would she do? It's not like there were similar nongovernmental organizations (NGOs) on every corner with HELP WANTED signs out. Her experience was precise; comparable opportunities were bound to be rare—and distant. She'd have to sell the house—how long would that take? Should she list it now, or might she then end up with nothing—no job, no house . . . no future, no life, no hope? It was all too much. She muffled a sob and drifted into the dark relief of exhausted sleep.

Three weeks had passed since . . . *It* . . . had happened. The horror and grief were still fresh and raw, but fear was starting to eclipse them. Shanti was only just starting to grasp how difficult it would be to find a new job anywhere with nearly her old position's pay and influence, even if she could find something in her field of expertise and interest. She was trying to live frugally, but how long could her savings last?

That's when the idea of the victory garden came to her. She had heard family stories about her grandparents' victory garden that sustained them during the hard times of World War II. It had been the inspiration for one of her most innovative and successful programs at the NGO—improving the health and the future of impoverished families around the world by teaching them about and providing the tools needed to grow healthful, life-sustaining vegetables. It seemed like a small thing, but it made a huge difference.

Starting her own victory garden seemed like a good idea, although Shanti's future was so uncertain she didn't know if she'd still be around by harvest. It was just as likely that by the time her vegetables had ripened, she'd still be there—totally broke—and they'd be the only things between her and starvation. Besides, buying forty-nine-cent packets of vegetable seeds would give her an excuse to get out, go to the store, and actually buy something without feeling guilty. As luck would have it, it was just the right time to start seeds indoors. Shanti felt her first glimmer of hope.

The victory garden had been more difficult than Shanti had imagined. She wondered if the people her program helped in Africa and Indonesia had felt the same way. Seeds didn't cost forty-nine cents anymore, she discovered. And you needed things like peat pots and soil just to get started. Then, to keep seedlings from getting spindly, she'd needed special grow-light bulbs that she'd installed in the fluorescent light over the worktable in the garage.

And the garden spot had its own issues. Although years earlier she'd had a small garden, her all-consuming job and hectic travel schedule had left her little time to tend it. It had long since filled with grass. She had to reclaim it—and expand it—with hard work and grim determination . . . and the sharp end of a pickax. Almost every swing she took met rock—enough eventually to ring her garden in a decent border. Shanti found something cathartic in the fierce blows necessary to create the garden. As her muscles ached more, her heart ached a little less.

In spite of the chilly early-spring weather, most days Shanti worked several hours on making her garden. With the rocks removed, the soil was half a foot lower than the grass, and the dense clay desperately needed amending—compost, peat, manure, topsoil—anything would be an improvement. She hadn't counted on that expense, but the seedlings were growing well, and she didn't want to give up on the investment she'd already made in money, time, and hope. She still had few promising leads on the job front—and scant emotional fortitude to pursue them. It felt more imperative than ever that she make this garden produce.

Shanti felt a measure of satisfaction as she sowed the seeds of her early-spring crop—lettuce, spinach, radishes, carrots, and onions. Her gratification grew when it came time to transplant the specimens she had nurtured from tiny seeds to sturdy, healthy plants in her garage. But an unexpected stab of sorrow pierced her heart as she prepared to transplant her tomatoes into the garden. Carefully following instructions, she had sown several seeds into each pot to be sure at least one would grow. But several of the pots held two successful plants—equally large, healthy, and full of potential. Shanti considered planting them as they were but knew both plants would suffer from being so close to each other. The correct thing to do would be to "thin" them down to just one plant per pot. She could barely stand to do it, but she plucked up her resolve and pulled them out.

Suddenly Shanti saw herself in the discarded plants: They had done nothing wrong. They didn't deserve to die. One minute they had been happily growing in the spot they'd been comfortably planted; the next they'd been cruelly uprooted and left, exposed, to slowly wither and die. Didn't they deserve a chance to live, grow, and thrive as much as the others? Maybe more so. This felt personal. Shanti felt desolate.

But then she had a thought. She scooped up the drooping tomato plants, clumps of dirt still clinging to their bare roots, and carried them to the front yard. This year she couldn't afford the bright pink geraniums she customarily bought for the planters that flanked the front door. She'd plant the beleaguered tomatoes in the flower boxes for now. She didn't feel too hopeful about their chances for survival, but she was determined that they'd at least have the chance. Then it would be up to them.

The garden was coming along nicely. Every day after checking out the job openings at Monster.com, sending out résumés, and following leads, Shanti inspected and tended her garden.

She had to admit it was progressing better than the job hunt. She still felt emotionally and physically savaged from the unfathomable, unfair, unfixable blow she'd been dealt three months earlier. She still felt she'd never heal, never get her life back on track, or be happy again.

But Shanti was starting to notice something that amazed and thrilled her. The damaged little tomato plants she'd first uprooted and then planted in the geranium boxes—the plants she'd identified with emotionally—went beyond merely surviving: they started to thrive. For the first few days Shanti hadn't been sure they'd live. For the first few weeks they were stunted, their rate of growth far behind that of the garden tomatoes. But after that the traumatized little plants had taken off.

Now they were nearly twice the size of the others and had thicker, healthier branches loaded with many times the tomatoes, and of a much larger size. Although they looked a bit out of place in her flower boxes, each day it became more apparent that this new, sunny, south-side location was by far the superior spot for growing tomatoes. The realization brought a thrill of hope and comprehension. Was it possible that her own painful situation might likewise turn out to be for her good? Like these tomatoes, could it be that she had left a place that held no future for her and had been compassionately transplanted to a place where, in time, she might actually become even more fruitful? The idea spurred her imagination. Maybe she wasn't thinking largely enough. Maybe God had allowed this painful thing to happen to her as a new opportunity for growth and fruitfulness.

It may have been a small thing, but it made a world of difference. For the first time in many months—no, years—the future felt exciting.

The November air was crisp as Shanti left home that morning. Although the garden had frozen several weeks earlier, she was pleased to note that the flower-box tomatoes, elevated several feet off the ground, had escaped the killing freeze and were still growing, the staked limbs bowed with the weight of ripening fruit. *Just like my life*, she mused.

It had been a hard summer, but a fruitful one. She'd had lots of fresh vegetables, enough to eat and still can twenty-eight pints of tomatoes, fourteen quarts of pickles, and ten pints of beets. She'd lost twenty pounds and regained the spring in her step.

Best of all, she had taken inventory of her life—her experience and connections, her passions and gifts—and then put the innovation and can-do attitude that were hallmarks of her service at the NGO to work on her own behalf. Everything had fallen into place for her to start her own nonprofit program that expanded on those she'd instituted earlier. Only this time she was running things her way—without the roadblocks from small-minded people who hindered progress and buried potential.

It was off to a good start, and the possibilities seemed limitless. Would she produce as much fruit as the uprooted tomatoes that had inspired her? Shanti had faith—and determination—that she would.

Chapter 5

Cultivating Friendships

*T*rust in Me and do good to others. Cultivate faithfulness. Daily plant seeds of encouragement in others' lives. Friendships increase your potential. They come to your rescue when life isn't fun or when you falter. Friends stick by you in times of need, and a friend's counsel is sweet to the soul.

Abiding with you,
Your King and Friend

—*from Psalm 37:3; Hebrews 3:13;*
Ecclesiastes 4:9–10; Proverbs 17:17, 27:9

Everyone who undertakes gardening understands the importance of planting and harvesting. They're the bookends on the garden experience. But true gardeners recognize that much of what determines the success of any crop—vegetables or flowers—happens somewhere in the middle. Cultivating aerates and loosens compact soil, making it easier for plants to breathe. It also dispatches pesky weeds that could choke out more desirable plants, stealing nutrients from the soil and space needed by the plants to grow to their full potential.

Gardens aren't the only living things we must cultivate. Everyone loves the bountiful reward we reap from having good friends—sharing dreams and secrets, deep conversations and fun times; rejoicing in one another's victories; and knowing friends will be there when you need them. But sometimes we overlook the importance of cultivating friendships. With the hectic pace of modern life and the isolation that technology brings—automated tellers, answering machines, even online shopping—it's easy to overlook the little things that build and nurture friendships.

What can you do to cultivate friendships, old and new? Here are a few reminders:

- Spend quality time together.
- Put your friends' needs before your own when appropriate.
- Do something thoughtful.
- Keep in touch.
- Defend your friends.
- Speak highly of them.
- Laugh with them.
- Love them.

Treat everyone you meet as a potential pal. You never know who God might send into your life to be a friend.

Friends are flowers in life's garden.

Source unknown

Amigos

"Syd, stop!" Anneliese said firmly, taking her briefcase from him and resting her hand lightly on his chest before quickly kissing his cheek. "Enough with the advice. I'm a grown woman. I've been at this company for eleven years—manager for seven. I know how to handle problem employees. Trust me."

"I do trust you," her husband said glumly. "I guess I'm just jealous."

"Jealous? You want to fire someone? Because if anyone should be jealous, it's me." She toed his slippers with the point of her high-heeled shoe. "I wouldn't mind being able to stay home and do anything I felt like."

"But that's just it." Syd dropped his gaze to the floor. "I can't do what I feel like doing. I miss the office. I miss being in charge, using my mind, solving problems. Once in a while I'd like to feel the adrenaline rush that comes from grappling with an unexpected problem—rising to meet the challenge. I want to deal with people, bright people—people who look at me with respect, knowing I have something valuable to say, not like I'm some worn-out old guy who goes for coffee by himself at midday, who merits no more conversation than, 'Do you want fries with that?'"

Anneliese looked at her watch. "I'm sorry, but I absolutely can't be late today. Why don't you give Don a call and take him to lunch?"

"Atlanta on business—again."

"Lyle?"

Syd shook his head. He wouldn't tell her, but he'd never call Lyle again. When he'd stepped down as CEO, he'd quickly discovered who his real friends were—and who they weren't.

Anneliese kissed his lips tenderly, then opened the door. "Don't let it get you down," she encouraged him above the noise of the garage door's rising. "I've been praying that God will send you a friend."

With that she was gone, and the day was his alone once again.

He scooped up the lunch he'd made for her and headed to the kitchen. She'd been right—salami with peppers and onions did sound more like his taste than hers. He opened the fridge, hesitating a moment as he inspected its contents. "*Ehhhhh,*" he noised resignedly, drawing back and shutting the door. He pulled the sandwich from the bag, threw the rest onto the table, and made his way to the garage, taking large bites of the aromatic sandwich. The doctor wouldn't approve, but then why should the doctor be the only one to get what he wants?

When Dr. Rosenthal scared him into taking early retirement, Syd had at first been grateful for the warning—and compliant with the doctor's lifestyle change recommendations. The perilously high blood pressure that wouldn't come down, the heart palpitations that had alarmed him during several critical acquisition meetings, and the third recurrence of his bleeding ulcer had made real the doctor's dire predictions of an early grave if he didn't give up his high-powered, high-stress job.

It hadn't been bad at first. Probably in part because it hadn't seemed permanent but more like a well-deserved vacation. He'd kept in touch with his old colleagues, who continued treating him with deferential respect. But as the weeks turned into months, he'd gradually found them less accessible and himself outside the loop. They had fewer questions, sought his advice less . . . actually seemed impatient with his questions and suggestions. He had not anticipated the painful transition from powerful man to one of little consequence—or purpose.

Syd kicked off his slippers and pulled on his work boots. Around his waist over his green-and-black-checked flannel shirt he tied a bright orange canvas belt with pockets and loops laden with all kinds of tools—bypass pruner, knife, garden shears, kneeling pads, digging fork, and trowel. He was distressed when his leather gloves were not in their designated spot in his fastidiously organized workspace and muttered softly as he pulled out a clear plastic container about the size of a shoebox and rummaged through a host of mismatched garden gloves of all colors and sizes before thinking to check in the pocket of his apron.

"There you are," he grunted, slipping them on. He held up his hands and inspected them. "Let's get to work, boys."

"Good morning, Cindy," he called out as he hit the backyard. "Grandpa Ray . . . Camilla . . . Big John . . . Julia Child . . . Blushing June . . . my Darling Annabelle. I say, Queen Elizabeth!" Syd affected an English accent and bowed dramatically before a medium pink grandiflora rose. "I suppose you wonder why I've called you all to this meeting," Syd addressed the dozens of roses that graced his luxuriant, winding gardens. He chuckled to himself, then pulled out the pruner and started deadheading blossoms past their peak.

In the months following his retirement, Syd had chosen a

new hobby, growing roses, and pursued it with the relentless diligence that had made him a top-notch executive. He had painstakingly researched roses—planting, care, and varieties—before developing a "business" plan he had followed exactingly to create a garden of outstanding health and beauty. He took great pride in his accomplishment . . . still, it felt lonely. Roses had no words, not even William Shakespeare or Charles Dickens.

Woof! Woof woof woof!

Syd was startled by the sudden presence of a big, black dog. "Not you again. What are you doing here? Go home. Go home!"

But the dog did not go home. Instead, he picked up something and brought it to Syd, dropping it in front of a deep pink hybrid tea rose. With irony, Syd noted the rose's name: Friendship. The dog had brought another "gift" of friendship—a woman's cloth garden glove with stripes of many colors. This was the seventh such offering in the past month. Syd picked it up, trying to avoid touching the spots made wet by the big dog's mouth. "Where are you getting these?" Syd demanded. "Why bring them to me? The neighbors will think I'm a thief!"

Syd reached for the dog's collar and tags, but without his reading glasses, he couldn't tell what they said. The dog thought Syd was trying to pet him: he wagged his tail, wiggled happily, and rubbed his head against Syd's gloved hand. "You like gloves, do you?" Syd felt his heart softening toward the interloper. For the first time, he noticed how thin the dog was. "Doesn't your owner feed you, boy?" Syd removed his glove and scratched behind the dog's ears.

The mystery had piqued his interest. Perhaps, if he applied his CEO problem-solving skills, he could solve the enigma of the dog and the garden gloves. He relished the challenge.

"Good heavens," the plump, pleasant-looking woman exclaimed gleefully. "That's my garden glove! What's it doing in your tree?" She looked curiously from the line of gloves, clipped to a tree limb with clothespins, to the sign that said Is ONE YOURS? and then to Syd, who sat on his front steps. The black dog lounged a few feet away in the shade of the dogwood.

"Apparently, this dog has an affinity for garden gloves."

"Your dog stole my glove?" The woman put her hand to her chest in a gesture of surprise.

"He's not my dog. I was hoping someone would know who he is and where he belongs."

She peered over her glasses at the dog. "Kuenzes on the corner have a black dog, but she's much smaller. Midgie, I think . . . that looks like old Mr. Zook's dog."

"Mr. Zook?" Syd asked hopefully. "Where does Mr. Zook live?"

"Honey, Mr. Zook died in March. His grandson is getting the house—one block over—ready to sell, but I don't think he wanted the dog. One of the first things he did was take out the doghouse."

Syd felt his anger rising on the dog's behalf.

"Imagine that dog taking my glove and bringing it to you," she chattered on as she plucked an orange-and-yellow-flowered glove from the branch. "I didn't even know anyone lived in this house until last summer when you planted your beautiful rose bushes. Is that when you moved in?"

"When I retired," Syd corrected. "Before that, my wife, Anneliese, and I kept pretty busy—my name is Syd, by the way. Syd Farraday."

"I'm Magda," she responded. "Magda Ruiz. My husband is thinking of retiring in a year or so. Maybe you'd have some advice that would help him make up his mind," she asked hopefully.

"More than happy to talk with him," Syd assured her, smiling. "The white-brick house? You have some lovely roses. Are they Peace?"

"Why yes," Magda seemed surprised. "I was pruning them when my glove vanished." She laughed. "They're doing a lot better than my roses out back. The neighbor behind me, Leo Haynes, grows roses, too. He said it's something called black spot, but I can't seem to get rid of it, and the leaves are all dropping."

"Wait a minute," Syd responded. "I have something you should try."

When Anneliese came home late that evening, Syd didn't get up to meet her. He didn't want to wake the dog, who was lying next to him on the couch, his head in Syd's lap. In response to the shocked look on Anneliese's face, Syd said, "Don't worry, I gave him a bath."

"Who is he?" Anneliese asked. "Where did he come from? Is that the garden-glove thief?"

"Uh-huh," Syd grunted affirmatively.

"Doesn't he belong to someone?" she asked, concerned.

"Yep," Syd answered, "me."

"What do you mean, 'me'?" Anneliese's voice registered disbelief. She sat next to Syd and groped through the dog's fur, looking for tags.

"I mean he's my new friend. You prayed God would send me a friend. Well, here he is. Oh, and by the way, I met a few of the neighbors this afternoon. We're starting a neighborhood garden society." He grinned. "I'm president."

She smiled, holding out the tag toward Syd. "Did you see this?"

He reached across the coffee table to retrieve his reading glasses. He placed them on his nose and couldn't help but laugh when he read the name on the tag: Amigo.

Chapter 6

Pest Control

*D*on't be surprised when things don't go as planned. Trouble is a normal part of life. Don't be fooled—the enemy is on a mission to steal and destroy your life. Instead of caving in to pressure to conform, offer your life to Me as a living sacrifice. Be transformed by renewing your mind. Seek My good, pleasing, and perfect will for you on a daily basis. Stay the course. Run with endurance the path I've marked out for you. Pull out the "weeds" in your life. Get rid of the things that hinder you and prevent you from becoming all I created you to be as you focus on Me.

Giving you strength to patiently endure,
Your God of Abundant Life

—*John 16:33, 10:10; Romans 12:1–2; Hebrews 12:1–2*

Aphids. Thrips. Japanese beetles. Squash bugs. Grasshoppers. Slugs. Nematodes. Caterpillars. Vine borers. Cut worms. Rabbits. Moles. Squirrels. Raccoons. Mice. Lots of pests are enemies of the gardener. They'll strip a plant bare, burrow into fruit, sap the strength or the life from a vine, or steal your harvest—even entire rows of plants! No gardener is immune to the ravages of such garden pests. It's a frustrating, inevitable part of growing things—a constant battle to be waged.

Interruptions. Distractions. Insufficient resources and time. Problems, big and small. Miscommunication. Conflicting priorities. Constant demands. Exhaustion. Selfishness. These pests are a few of the enemies of our families. They crop up from day to day, demanding our attention until we can focus on nothing else. Pest prevention.

Damage control. We bustle about doing all the things demanded of us while we lose sight of what's truly important—the people—our children, our spouses, our parents, our dearest friends.

When we start to resent or grow weary of those we love because of what they demand of us, watch out! We just might be in danger of losing our perspective, of seeing as a pest something of great and irreplaceable value. You can view a petunia in the midst of an onion patch either as a weed or as a marvelous surprise—an unexpected blessing to be embraced and treasured. It depends on your perspective—and your priorities.

Are you besieged by pests? Make sure your priorities are in order. Only then can you recognize what's truly important and know what to let slide.

*What is a weed? A plant whose virtues
have not yet been discovered.*

Ralph Waldo Emerson

Days to Maturity

July 9: forty-nine days until the first day of school. Laurie groaned miserably. Would she be able to hold out? Maybe not. "Dylan, did I give you permission to take your Game Boy apart? Put it back together right now, before you forget where each part came from."

"Chase! Stop drumming. It's so loud I can't hear myself think!" Laurie pressed a hand to her weary head. The noise grew softer but didn't stop. "Hailey, did you spill batter in the oven again? I smell something burning!"

"That's not my cake," eleven-year-old Hailey protested. "It's Samantha's experiment. I think she discovered some sort of acid—the plastic spoon melted. Cool!"

"Samantha!" Laurie raced for the kitchen. "Please be care— Oh, my goodness!" she gasped. "This place is a wreck! Hailey, you promised me you'd clean up the kitchen when you were done!"

"I did clean it," Hailey said defensively. She rubbed a glop of batter she'd missed off the counter and pushed a pile of dirty bowls back from the edge.

"This is *not* clean," Laurie fumed, taking a test tube from Samantha's hand and steering her toward the sink to wash up. "Enough!" She whistled shrilly through her teeth. "Kids, everyone . . . front and center . . . NOW!"

When she finally had the kids—Hailey, Dylan, and the quads: eight-year-olds Chase, Jessica, Ashley, and Samantha— settled in the family room watching *Over the Hedge*, Laurie left the mess and chaos behind to make her own escape "over the hedge." Lately it seemed the garden was the only place she could relax and find peace. She took deep breaths and tried to decompress as she put on her garden clogs and tied the apron with the shears and all the pockets around her waist, heading for the small plot of earth where she nurtured her soul.

She briefly imagined Clay relaxing on a beach somewhere with his new "child," his nubile twenty-three-year-old new wife. Laurie consciously pushed it from her mind as she felt the bitterness rising again. How beautiful and appealing would Shana be with another twelve years and six kids to her credit?

Clay had never been the responsible type or much help on the home front—especially since their third child had unexpectedly turned out to be their fourth, fifth, and sixth children as well—but this was her first summer completely alone with the kids. And it was driving her to the edge! She was counting down the days to the end of summer vacation. Even her high-paced office job at the local college seemed appealing, since there she actually got to sit down.

The garden had been her escape. She took out her aggression on hapless weeds. The fresh smell of the dirt revived her, and seeing new growth gave her a sense of progress and hope. Looking forward to a harvest made her feel that all her hard work was worth it: the produce was the reward she needed to draw her back day after day. Today she could practically taste the green beans she knew were ready for harvest.

"Hey, what's this?" She knew instantly that something had messed with her beans. Leaves had been stripped and, on closer inspection, she found teeth marks on half-eaten beans. Anger just below the surface quickly boiled up. Was this, too, to be ruined? She knew instantly that the culprit was a rabbit.

"Couldn't you at least have eaten whole beans—and fewer?" Laurie railed into the air. It reminded her of the kids leaving half-full cans of warm, flat pop on the counter and then opening another. But this was worse. She couldn't just go to the store and buy another case of homegrown beans.

"You're not going to get the best of me, rabbit!" Laurie warned as she headed into the house. Cayenne pepper might help.

July 16: forty-two days till the first day of school. These days weren't getting any easier. Laurie was pretty sure she'd have to repaint the girls' bedroom after the purple house that Ashley painted on the wall that morning while her mom was taking a shower had made her see red. She had then resorted to a tactic she disliked: bribery. She told the kids that if they quietly played table games or read all afternoon, she'd take them for ice cream that night. She was desperate.

Her bad attitude went with her as she stalked to the garden to survey the latest damage. The cayenne pepper had failed to repel the hungry rabbit; likewise the pepper spray, pinwheels, scarecrow owl, and even the chicken-wire fence—the little thief had simply dug under and eaten a row of peas and the tops of some carrots. So now she would try the same tactic inspired by her kids: bribery.

She wasn't sure what this rotten rabbit would like better

than her garden, so she brought a variety of items: an apple, half a banana, lettuce leaves, and a carrot. As she neared the garden, something shot out of the asparagus patch—just a blur of motion. "You'd better run," Laurie taunted. "I'm onto you now!"

She scattered her offerings around the asparagus. "Here," she said in a sweet voice. "Good stuff, bunny. Wouldn't you rather eat this than my garden? Come and get it. Eat until there's no room for my veggies."

July 19: thirty-nine days till the first day of school. Laurie was heading to the garden earlier than usual, thanks to Jessica's early morning "Olympic swim." A sopping wet little girl in her bathing suit, goggles, and swim fins had stood dripping on her bedroom rug at 5:47 a.m., wanting to celebrate.

"Mommy, I won the gold medal in the butterfly!" Jessica had exulted breathlessly. Laurie hadn't felt like celebrating when she discovered what Jessica really meant. Awake early, Jessica had filled the tub with water, then splashed most of it out "practicing for the Olympics." Everything was soaked everywhere: the wallpaper, the rugs, and the toilet paper.

After drying off the little girl, she'd sent her back to bed with a strict warning against waking up anyone else. By the time she had cleaned up the bathroom, it was six thirty, and she thought it might be a good time to check on her garden. Laurie had an apple in her hand: by now she knew the rabbit didn't like lettuce and wouldn't touch baby carrots, although regular carrots were worth a nibble. But the rabbit's real passion seemed to be apples, and Laurie's bribes were at least partially successful in sating the rabbit's appetite and salvaging part of her harvest.

As she got to the door of her house, she paused a moment and looked out. What she saw stopped her cold. A rabbit—no, a bunny, scarcely larger than the palm of her hand—was in plain sight, chewing on a blade of grass, then slowly loping to munch on a frond of her potted asparagus fern. The smallness, the vulnerability of this, her enemy, surprised and immobilized her. She watched intently. How old was it? Where was its mother? Was it old enough to be on its own? Surely some other rabbit was ravaging her garden: this bunny was too small and cute to wreak such havoc.

The mottled gray rabbit was white at both ends, with a cottontail and blaze of white on its forehead that only endeared it more to Laurie. But the last icy spot in her heart melted when she saw what it did next. It leaped in the air and spun around as if for joy, then ran along the patio before leaping and twisting again and running back. It seemed to be practicing running, and it exuded such ecstasy—at the beauty of the morning, the warmth of the new day, the euphoria of life—that Laurie was transfixed . . . and transformed.

When was the last time she'd felt like that? She couldn't even remember.

August 7: one day until the kids would return from ten days with Grandpa Phil and Grandma Nancy; six days since she'd last seen her bunny. She'd been looking forward to some peaceful time alone, but the past few days had been fairly miserable. Of all the stupid things; she felt unexplainable loss, sadness, and loneliness. She had gotten up early the last three days to stand watch at the back door, hoping to catch a repeat of the bunny's early morning escapades—or just to see him at all—but she'd had no luck.

Her garden had been unmolested for more than a week, her apple offerings uneaten. Laurie had planted more carrots, beans, and peas, hoping they might tempt the little guy out of hiding. And finally she had bought a bag of rabbit food at the garden store. Perhaps that would be more to his liking or would at least help her see some evidence of his continued existence. She couldn't bear the thought of him being eaten by a hawk or hit by a car.

But it was pointless to fool herself any longer. The bunny was gone. Her garden would grow in peace for the rest of the season. That should be a good thing. It was what she'd wanted. So why did she feel this way?

As she neared the garden, she was startled by movement in the asparagus patch. Her bunny buddy darted out, but not out of sight. He sat watching her, even as she watched him. Her jubilation melted into doubt. Could this really be her bunny? He looked so much bigger. The familiar white blaze on his forehead was fading. Still, he had been in his usual spot, and he seemed comfortable with her presence, as he had in the weeks before he disappeared. This must be him, but where had he been?

Moving slowly so she wouldn't startle him, she sat on the garden bench and watched him as she analyzed her feelings. Suddenly her cheeks felt hot with shame as she realized that her experience with the bunny was a microcosm of her struggles with her own lot in life. She had been focusing on the battles and missing out on the joys. Would her own children grow up as quickly as this bunny had? Would she grieve to find she had missed their best days together, times of sharing their discoveries and rejoicing in their distinctive personalities and gifts?

Suddenly she could imagine them all grown up: Hailey a famous television baker, Dylan an electrical engineer, Chase the drummer for a chart-topping band, Samantha a Nobel Prize–winning scientist, Ashley a brilliant artist, and Jessica an Olympic-gold-medalist swimmer. A tear rolled down her cheek, and she felt her chest swell with pride. She didn't want to miss a single step along the way.

Oh my goodness, she realized. *It's August 7!* Just twenty days left until the first day of school. Only twenty days to sing along with Chase, go to the science museum with Dylan and Samantha, paint a mural on the sidewalk with Ashley, sign up for swimming lessons with Jessica, and experiment in the kitchen with Hailey. Only twenty days left to enjoy every minute of every day together. Laurie could hardly wait.

Chapter 7

Harvesting Your Crop

*D*on't lose heart in the midst of the struggles of life. If you quit, you'll miss out on the promised results. Trust me to make the pieces of the puzzle fit. You can be confident that I'll faithfully bring to fruition the good seeds I've planted in you. My harvest is abundant—it's just waiting for you and others to get involved in My plan.

Blessing you,
Your Lord of the Harvest

—*Galatians 6:9; Philippians 1:6; Luke 10:2*

Nothing beats the juicy flavor of a homegrown tomato. Next to them, store tomatoes are just cardboard-flavored imposters. The same goes for melt-in-your-mouth green beans; sweet, buttery corn right from the stalk; and peas so fresh they squeak when you snap them. Harvests like these are why most people get into gardening.

Admit it, don't you still tell stories about that year your strawberries produced one hundred quarts? Or the year your summer squash produced enough to single-handedly feed a small African nation? Don't you have pictures of your prize-winning watermelon? And who could blame you?

But every gardener experiences the other side of the harvest coin, too. Harvests take a huge investment of time, hard work, and even money. And many things beyond our control can make a harvest

disappointing. But true gardeners don't
let it shake them. They find new ways to
improve the soil and guard against extreme
elements and pests, and they redouble their
efforts.

What sort of harvest has disappointed you and
made you contemplate giving up? A friendship?
Learning a language? Getting in shape? Your
marriage? Keep at it. Many beautiful flowers
don't blossom in the first year. Give up too
soon and you'll miss their unique fragrance.
One tomato plant can produce hundreds of
fruits, while each onion set brings a harvest
of only one. Every plant is different. So is
every person, every situation.

Got a hard row to hoe? Don't give
up. "Let us not become weary in
doing good, for at the proper
time we will reap a harvest
if we do not give up"
(Galatians 6:9).

A good deed is never lost; he who sows courtesy reaps friendship, and he who plants kindness gathers love.

Basil

Many Happy Returns

"The latest harvest," Karen called out to her sister. She set the bag of yellow squash on the counter, shoving aside ten unmatched, drained coffee cups and half as many dirty plates. *About two days' worth, I'd guess.*

"Oh, thanks!" Jen's distracted voice emanated from some

distant part of the house. "I didn't hear you come in."

"It's okay, I can't stay. I have to pack."

Jen came up the stairs smelling like the can of spray adhesive in her hand. "I'm not finished with the McMurney presentation, and they want to see the new ad campaign Monday morning, so . . ."

Karen gave her sister a knowing look. "Uh-huh. And how close are you?"

Jen smirked and wrinkled her nose. "I kind of just started it this afternoon."

"Jen-ni-fer!"

"I know, I know." Jen raised her hands in mock surrender as she went to the coffeemaker. "Rats. Did you drink the last of this?"

Karen rolled her eyes. "No, I did not drink your coffee."

"I've been busy!" Jen gave the empty pot a quick rinse and filled it for a new brew. "Jason wanted to see a movie yesterday, and I had promised Lisa I'd help her pick out invitations, which I totally forgot until she called from the printer, and—oh! That reminds me, were you able to find the game I promised Ryan for his birthday, what was it called again?"

"Madden NFL, and yes, I got it." She dug the PlayStation 3 game out of her purse. "You know, you don't have to always get him the latest thing."

"Are you kidding? I'm the *cool* aunt," Jen said with a cocky but good-natured grin. "Anyway, can I pay you on Thursday, after I get my check?"

Jen still hadn't paid her for Ryan's Christmas gift.

"Oh—and do you have any of that wrapping paper left? I think I'm out."

Have you ever even purchased wrapping paper? Karen thought. "I think so." She paused, knowing what Jen was really getting at and wanting to make her wait for at least a fraction of a second before giving in. "Do you want me to drop it off later, or do you want me to just keep this and wrap it when I wrap our gifts?"

"Would you mind? Thanks!"

Karen avoided answering that pseudoquestion. "Okay. So the party is tomorrow at seven, and then we're leaving for the cottage Sunday morning."

"Right. I'll be there." Jen kissed her sister on the cheek. "Oh, and thanks again for the squash. How's the garden going?"

This was Jen's attempt to show interest and compensate for asking Karen to be her personal shopper. Jen was sincere, she was just . . . well . . . Jen. Karen let out a weary sigh. "Most of it's fine. I'll have more tomatoes for you tomorrow. I had to pick these today, because the vine borers have gotten to the squash plants, and they're dying."

"The what?"

"Vine borers. They burrow into the vine from underground, and whoosh, it's over. All that fertilizing, spraying, and picking off squash bugs by hand, for nothing. I've only gotten about two dozen squashes, counting these, from three plants. I think next year I'm just not going to bother." Karen felt her throat constrict and her eyes mist over, and she looked away. She loved gardening, and the occasional failed experiment was no reason to cry. *What's wrong with me lately?* "Anyway, all that time and effort for so little return . . . it's too discouraging."

"Bummer." Jen's voice registered sympathy. "I don't know how you can garden anyway. All that work, and all those bugs. How did you tell me to cook these again?"

The next day was Saturday, and while her husband, Paul, got their boat ready for the trip, Karen baked a cake, wrapped gifts, and hurriedly checked her list of things to do before the family left for vacation.

"Anything I can do to help in here?" Paul asked as she rounded the corner.

"Everything ready?"

"All we have to do now is fill the cooler and load the luggage. Hey!" he said, spying the basket of freshly picked tomatoes on the counter. "Nice!" He kissed her forehead, but Karen was terse as she sliced cucumbers for the dinner salad.

"Picked the last of the squash today."

"Yeah, I noticed the vines. Sorry." He gave her a squeeze of the shoulders. "Where are they?"

"Took them to *Jennifer*." The slicing got more aggressive. "I'd promised her some. Of course, that was before I knew they'd be my last. Do you think she'll even remember to use them?"

Paul chuckled but stifled it when she threw him a cold glare.

"Sorry. What's wrong?"

"Nothing." She came down hard with the knife.

"Uh-huh . . ."

Karen's shoulders sagged. "Judy called today." Judy was the friend who always took care of Karen's garden when the family took their annual vacation at the lake. "Something came up. She can't watch the garden."

"Well, how about Jen?"

"Jen?!" Karen slammed down the knife and whirled around. "My *sister* Jen?! The one who can't remember to show up for a dinner *she* scheduled? The person who relies on you to change the oil in her car and on me to do everything from shopping to scheduling flights and making sure she doesn't forget Mom's birthday?"

Paul raised his eyebrows.

Karen felt her temper deflate. "Sorry. It's not that I mind doing those things for her. It's just . . ."

"It'd be nice to get a little fruit from your labor?"

"It's not like I want an even return. It's just . . . it makes me feel sad, and then I get angry. I mean, I worked so hard to nurture those squash plants and keep the bugs away, and it's all for nothing, and then the little reward I do get, I give to Jen. I don't even know if she appreciates any of it." She rubbed her hand over her face. "And I do it because I love her, but . . ."

"She's like the squash plant," Paul interjected. "And for all your planting and tending, you get a rather pitiful harvest."

Karen frowned and felt the corners of her mouth quiver.

That was why the squash had bothered her so much. Why hadn't she seen the connection?

Paul put his arm around Karen, and when he spoke it was in the deep, soothing tone that always steadied her. "Look, you know she loves you. She's just kind of . . . um . . . flighty."

Karen couldn't help but laugh.

"You can't change her ways any more than you can stop the vine borers. You garden because you love it, even though sometimes plants don't fare well. You do things for your sister because you love her, even though your efforts don't always seem successful. It's not fair. It's just what you do."

Karen wiped a tear on the tea towel and nodded.

"Here, I'll finish this. Make a list of basic tasks for Jen. She can handle it. We'll call her to make sure she at least remembers to water. The rest we'll just deal with when we get back."

Karen felt herself tense up as Paul pulled their SUV and boat trailer into the driveway after the long trip home. She was dreading what she'd find in the garden after being gone for so long. She wondered what had survived and what had gone the way of the squash.

It was almost dusk, but Karen couldn't wait. She headed for the garden, turning on the spigot for the hose on the way. Surely the ground would be parched.

From a distance, it looked better than she'd expected. Up close, the soil still felt soft and almost moist. Karen started to relax. Maybe this wouldn't be the disaster she'd anticipated. In the fading light, she checked the root vegetables. Some bugs had nibbled at the leaves, but a little pepper spray would put a stop to that. The chicken wire was still in place, so the rabbits had been held at bay. Now, the tomatoes. She could see several ripening, but none past their prime. Had Jen picked some after all? She stepped in to pluck a few.

Hey, wait a minute. As she straightened up, the tomatoes seemed taller than she'd remembered. She looked up and caught a glimpse of something bright purple. She moved closer, standing on tiptoe.

It was a purple pipecleaner.

Karen looked more closely now. In the fading light she could just make out little specks of color—yellow, red, green, pink, white, and more purple—holding up dozens of fruit-laden tomato vines. She put her hand to her mouth and giggled at her sister's improvisation. *Well, it's creative.*

Karen gave a quick inspection of the rest of the garden. *Whaddya know: Jen came through after all.*

As she passed the potting shed, Karen caught sight of something that made her stop. On the outside workbench were small, shadowy figures. She stepped closer. There, in a neat little row, were five unmatched coffee cups . . . filled with dirt and boasting small but sturdy green leaves. *What on earth?* She squinted to make out the new growth.

They were squash plants!

For a moment she just stood there. She put her hands to her

face, still looking at the makeshift pots, and let the sobs come.

"Did I do something wrong?" Jen's hesitant voice came from behind her.

Startled, Karen stopped crying and started laughing. "No," she said, wiping her face with the back of her glove. She turned to her sister and smiled. "Are you kidding? Everything looks great!"

"Oh, whew!" Jen's face registered relief. "I had no clue what I was doing. I saw that you had tied up the tomatoes, but I couldn't find that green Velcro stuff, so I was making it up as I went. And I felt bad about your squashes, so I thought maybe you could give it another try. I'd hate to see you give up on something you love. Anyway, the shed was locked, so I just used some of my mugs." She put her hands on her hips and continued animatedly. "Did you know they actually sell squash seeds at regular stores? There's still enough time for a harvest, right? The guy said they'll bear fruit in about fifty days. . . ."

Karen just chuckled. The little squash plants had already produced more fruit than she'd ever expected. *Fruit indeed.*